Ben F₁

A Man with Many Talents

Mary Beth Crum

Contents

Introduction 2

Growing Up 4

Printing and Writing 6

Leaving Boston 8

Starting a Newspaper 10

Making the Almanac 12

Helping the Community 14

Inventing 16

Helping the United States 20

Introduction

Benjamin Franklin was a good swimmer, but he wanted to swim faster. One day he thought of an idea. Maybe paddles on his hands and feet would help him. The paddles were so heavy that he couldn't swim very far. Would a kite work as a sail? Yes! Holding the kite string, Benjamin made it safely to the other side of the pond.

Benjamin Franklin liked to improve on and experiment with many things. His inventions and ideas helped to make life better for many people.

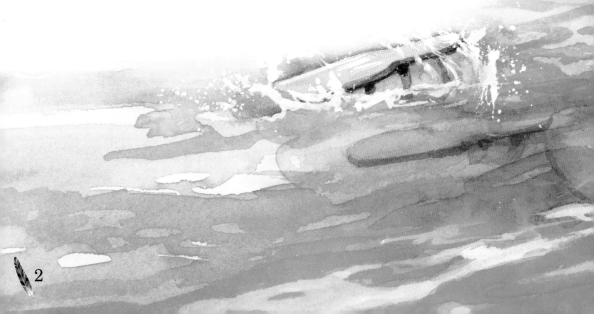

Benjamin tried to swim
faster, but the paddles
were too heavy.

Growing Up

Benjamin Franklin was born in Boston, Massachusetts, on January 17, 1706. He was the youngest son and the fifteenth child of Josiah Franklin. Josiah made soap and candles for a living, but he also liked to do experiments. He showed young Ben some of his science experiments.

Even though books were not always easy to get, Ben taught himself to read. Ben loved to read and learn as much as he could. Ben's father sent him to school when he was eight years old. Ben only went to school for two years because his parents couldn't pay for it any longer. But he continued learning on his own by reading many books.

Ann Child — **Josiah Franklin** — Abiah Folger

Elizabeth

Samuel

John

Hanna

Peter

Josiah

Mary

Anne

James

Joseph I

Sarah

Joseph II

Ebenezer

Thomas

Ben Franklin was from a large family.

Benjamin

Lydia

Jane

5

Printing and Writing

When Ben was 12, he helped his older brother James at his print shop. Ben often read late at night or early in the morning before the shop opened. He barely ate lunch so that he could read during his lunch hour.

Ben liked being around the printing presses.

James printed a newspaper called the
New England Courant at his print shop.
Readers were invited to write stories and
articles for the newspaper. Ben decided that
he wanted to write, too. He didn't think that
his brother would print anything that he
wrote, so he signed his writing Silence
Dogood, which was a girl's name. The funny
articles that he wrote were very popular.

THE   [Nº 80

New-England Courant.

From MONDAY February 4. to MONDAY February 11. 1723.

The late Publisher of this Paper, finding so many Inconveniences would arise by his carrying the Manuscripts and publick News to be supervis'd by the Secretary, as to render his carrying it on unprofitable, has intirely dropt the Undertaking. The present Publisher having receiv'd the following Piece, desires the Readers to accept of it as a Preface to what they may hereafter meet with in this Paper.

Non ego mordaci distrinxi Carmine quenquam,
Nulla venenato Litera onista Joco est.

LONG has the Press groan-
ed in bringing forth an
hateful, but numerous
Brood of Party Pamphlets,
malicious Scribbles, and
Billinigate Ribaldry. The
Rancour and bitterness it
has unhappily infused into
Mens minds, and to what
a Degree it has sowred
and leaven'd the Tempers
of Persons formerly esteem-
med some of the most
sweet and affable, is too
well known here, to need

eny further Proof or Representation of the Matter.
No generous and impartial Person then can blame the
present Undertaking, which is designed purely for the Diver-
sion and Merriment of the Reader. Pieces of Pleasancy
and Mirth have a secret Charm in them to allay the Heats
and Tumours of our Spirits, and to make a Man forget his
restless Resentments. They have a strange Power to tune the
harsh Disorders of the Soul, and reduce us to a serene and
placid State of Mind.
The main Design of this Weekly Paper will be to enter-

Four Pounds for the Pourtraiture. However, tho' this double
Face has spoilt us of a pretty Picture
fee old *Janus* in our Company.
     There is no Man in *Boston* better
for a *Couranteer*, or if you please,
Man of such remarkable *Opticks*,
once.
     As for his Morals, he is a chearly
Phrase expresses it. A Man of
Deportment, found Judgment; a m
Foppery, Formality, and endless C
     As for his Club, they aim at
Honour, than the Publick be ma
utmost of their Ambition to atten
ble good Offices to good Old *Jar*
and always will be the Readers hu
     P. S.   Gentle Readers, we deii
without a Latin Motto if we can
carries a Charm in it to the Vul
the pleasure of Construing. W
World with a Greek scrap or t
Types, and therefore we intreat
impute the defect to our Ignor
all the Greek Letters by heart.

His Majesty's Speech to the Parliament, October 11.
tho' already publish'd, may perhaps be new to many of
our Country Readers; we shall therefore insert it in this
Day's Paper.

His MAJESTY's most Gracious SPEECH
to both Houses of Parliament, on Thurs-
day October 11. 1722.
My Lords and Gentlemen,
I Am sorry to find my self obliged, at the Opening of
this Parliament, to acquaint you, That a dangerous
Conspiracy has for some time formed, and is still carrying on
against my Person and Government, in Favour of a Popish

Ben Franklin used
the name Silence
Dogood when he
wrote letters for his
brother's newspaper.

7

Leaving Boston

Some people in the colonies, which were areas ruled by the British, didn't like what James Franklin printed in the *New England Courant.* He often printed stories that went against the British government. James was even thrown into jail because of his stories!

James and Ben did not get along after James got out of jail, so Ben decided to leave Boston. On September 25, 1723, Ben got on a ship to New York. He could not find a job in New York, so he went all the way to Philadelphia, Pennsylvania.

Many people traveled by ship.

Ben traveled across several colonies before he settled in Philadelphia, Pennsylvania.

Starting a Newspaper

Ben lived with the Read family when he got to Philadelphia, and he became friends with the Reads' daughter, Deborah. Ben was a hardworking young man who wanted to start his own printing business.

Soon Ben married Deborah Read and bought his own printing shop. He sold writing paper, pens, ink, candles, and books. Ben wanted to start a newspaper that told people real news. *The Pennsylvania Gazette* was published by Ben, and it became the most popular newspaper in the area.

Ben Franklin wrote about news of the colonies.

Pennſylvania GAZETTE.

Containing the freſheſt Advices Foreign and Domeſtick.

From November 10. to November 17. 1737.

To the AUTHOR of the Pennſylvania GAZETTE.

SIR,

Ben opened his
own printing shop.

11

Making the Almanac

Ben decided to write a book called an almanac. Almanacs often had calendars, poems, and facts about the weather. While Ben predicted the weather from what he saw outside, people today use computers and satellites to be more accurate. He also wrote interesting sayings in his almanac, which are still famous today.

Here are some well-known sayings from Ben's almanac.

What do you think these sayings mean?

A penny saved is a penny earned.

An apple a day keeps the doctor away.

Early to bed and early to rise makes a man healthy, wealthy, and wise.

EARLY TO BED AND EARLY TO RISE, MAKES A MAN HEALTHY, WEALTHY, AND WISE.

This is a satellite image from space showing weather.

Helping the Community

Ben wanted to help his community. He created a club where people met to talk about how to make their community a better place. The club started the area's first library so that people could read more books. The club also started the first fire department, improved the streets, and put up streetlights.

Ben Franklin was also a firefighter.

A statue of Ben Franklin is now in front of the Pennsylvania Hospital.

Ben was upset that sick people didn't have a place to get help, so he started the Pennsylvania Hospital in 1751. It is still a hospital that people use today.

Inventing

Ben liked to think of easier ways to do things. When he was a boy, he invented paddles to help him swim faster, but they were too heavy. Today lighter paddles, called fins, are used for deep sea diving. Ben wanted his house to be warmer, so he invented a stove to heat it. He also invented a stepstool that he could use to reach things in his store. Ben also made special eyeglasses so that he only had to use one pair of glasses to see both up close and far away.

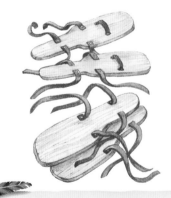
Ben tried to swim faster with these paddles but they didn't work.

Ben invented the Franklin stove.

More inventions by Ben Franklin:

1. Ben invented an instrument to measure how far his carriage had traveled, still used in cars today.

2. He also invented a chair that had a small table attached to it, later used in schools.

The top and bottom of Franklin's glasses were for seeing different distances.

Ben is most remembered for his experiments with electricity. Ben believed that lightning held electricity that people could use. One story says that Ben flew a kite with a key on it during a storm. When lightning struck the key, Ben felt a shock in his hand. Ben believed that the key got the electricity from the lightning.

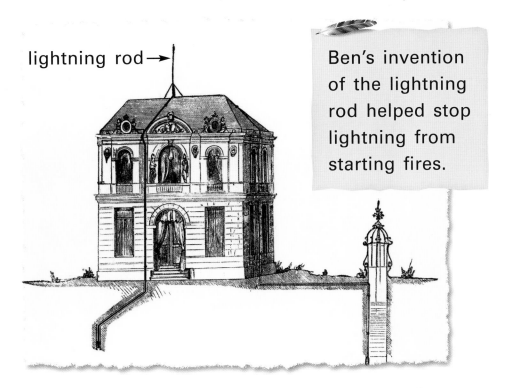

lightning rod →

Ben's invention of the lightning rod helped stop lightning from starting fires.

At that time, house fires often started when hot lightning hit a roof. Ben created the lightning rod that was placed on top of houses to help solve this problem. When lightning hit the metal rod, the electricity traveled to the ground instead of starting a fire in the house. One day Ben saw how useful his invention was when lightning struck his own house. The lightning rod saved Ben's home from danger!

Helping the United States

In 1776 the people in the 13 colonies wrote a letter to the King of England asking for independence. Ben helped write this letter, which was called the Declaration of Independence. Ben also helped write the Constitution of the United States in 1787, which helped form our government.

Benjamin Franklin died on April 17, 1790. He always thought of himself as just a printer, but he was much more than that to the rest of the world. Ben Franklin will always be remembered for his inventions that improved people's lives and for his belief in freedom. He was a man with many talents.

Benjamin Franklin helped to write the Declaration of Independence and the Constitution of the United States.

Time Line of Ben Franklin

Ben Franklin is born in Boston.

Ben leaves Boston to find work.

Ben marries Deborah Read.

1706

1718

1719

1728

1730

1733

Ben works as a printer's helper.

Ben starts his own newspaper, *The Pennsylvania Gazette.*

Ben's almanac is first printed.

Ben invents the Franklin stove.

Ben signs the Declaration of Independence.

Ben Franklin dies at age 84.

1741

1752

1776

1787

1790

Ben flies a kite in a thunderstorm and proves that lightning makes electricity.

Ben helps write the Constitution of the United States.

Index

almanac 12–13
Constitution 20–21
Declaration of Independence 20–21
electricity 18, 19
invention 2–3, 16–17, 19, 20
lightning 18–19
newspaper 7, 8, 10